STEEL DRUMMING AT THE APOLLO

THE ROAD TO SUPER TOP DOG

BY TRISH MARX

PHOTOGRAPHS BY ELLEN B. SENISI

LEE & LOW BOOKS INC.
NEW YORK

Acknowledgments

We would like to thank John Joseph, Philip Morris, Pat Harman, Jason Hyatt, Jeff Janiszewski, Peg Normandin, Susan Cohen, Rachel Gayne, Frank Serrano, Jessica Serrano, Tania Carkner, Wanda Byrd, Spencer Anderson, Sr., Felicia Terrell, Yvonne Williams, Kathy Sharpton, and Joyce Cachojas for their help with this project.

Thanks to The Gazette Newspapers, Schenectady, New York; reporter Philip Schwartz; and photographer Meredith L. Kaiser for permission to reproduce the article "Hamilton Hill Steel Drummers are heading to Harlem theater" on p. 39.

Thanks also to Andre Brown for his help with the copy on "Making Beats" and for acting as our contact with the group, communicating details, and helping to coordinate scheduling for photograph sessions and interviews.

And a very special thanks to the staff of the Apollo Theater Foundation, Inc.; Billy Mitchell, tour director at the Apollo Theater; Charles Sommer, legal counsel for the Apollo Theater; Miki Conn and the Hamilton Hill Arts Center; John Sayles School of Fine Arts, Schenectady, New York, City School District; Proctors Theater; and the awesome Spencer, Ahmel, Aaron, Andre, Steven, Dayshawn, and Dha'Sean, and their families.

—T.M. and E.B.S.

Author's Sources

Baker, Kevin. "Jitterbug Days," *New York Times,* January 22, 2006, sec. 14.

Cooper, Ralph, and Steve Dougherty. *Amateur Night at the Apollo: Ralph Cooper Presents Five Decades of Great Entertainment.* New York: HarperCollins, 1990.

Cox, Clinton. "The Apollo Theater: Where Great Singers and Comics Learned Their Trade," *New York Daily News,* July 22, 1973.

Eyerman, Ron, and Andrew Jamison. *Music and Social Movements: Mobilizing Traditions in the Twentieth Century.* New York: Cambridge University Press, 1998.

Fox, Ted. *Showtime at the Apollo: The Story of Harlem's World Famous Theater.* rev. ed. Rhinebeck, New York: Mill Road Enterprises, 2003.

Goldscheider, Eric. "On Amateur Night, the spotlight can singe," *Boston Globe,* June 19, 2005, Travel section.

Selvin, Joel. "Apollo Theater Stars Born at Zellerbach: Amateur Night Road Show Stops in Town to Pick Through a Hundred Hopefuls," *San Francisco Chronicle.* December 16, 2002, sec. D.

Photograph Credits

Wanda Byrd: Ahmel Williams as a young boy, p. 9; Family of Aaron Williams: Aaron Williams as a young boy, p. 13; Family of Spencer Anderson: Spencer Anderson as a young boy with his father and Aaron, p. 17; Felicia Terrell: Dayshawn Mojica as a young boy with his brother, p. 21; Angela Williams: Andre Brown as a young boy, p. 25; Kate Senisi: Steven Senisi playing electric bass, p. 31; Tania Carkner: Dha'Sean Serrano as a young boy with his brother, p. 33; Jessica Serrano: Hamilton Hill Steel Drum Band performing at Proctors Theater, p. 38; Alvin R. Peters: Hamilton Hill Steel Drum Band performing at New York State Legislature, p. 39; Kate Senisi: Hamilton Hill Steel Drum Band performing at Apollo Theater: bottom left, second right, and fourth right, p. 53.

Above photographs used with permission. All other photographs taken by Ellen B. Senisi. Many pictures were shot without flash at high-speed settings (1600 and 3200 ISO) because flash was not allowed or would have been distracting to the performers.

The phrase "where stars are born and legends are made," used on p. 40, is a trademark of the Apollo Theater Foundation, Inc.

LEE & LOW BOOKS Inc., 95 Madison Avenue, New York, NY 10016   leeandlow.com
Manufactured in China by Jade Productions, July 2015
Book design by HAVOC Media Design
Book production by The Kids at Our House
The text is set in ITC Cheltenham and News Gothic
(hc) 10 9 8 7 6 5 4 3 2 1
(pb) 10 9 8 7 6 5 4 3 2 1
First Edition
Library of Congress Cataloging-in-Publication Data
Marx, Trish.
Steel drumming at the Apollo : the road to super top dog / by Trish Marx ; photographs by Ellen B. Senisi. — 1st ed.
p. cm.
Summary: "Photo-essay about a high school steel drum band from upstate New York that participated in a series of talent competitions for a chance to win Super Top Dog on Amateur Night at the Apollo Theater in Harlem. Includes a CD of the band performing"— Provided by publisher.
ISBN 978-1-60060-124-8 (hc) ISBN 978-1-62014-231-8 (pb)
1. Hamilton Hill Steel Drum Band—Pictorial works. 2. Musicians—New York—Schenectady—Pictorial works. 3. Apollo Theatre (New York, N.Y.) I. Senisi, Ellen B. II. Title.
ML421.H35M37 2007   785'.68097471—dc22   2007008947

For Barb, with love
—T.M.

For the love of music and for the seven unique
musicians in the Hamilton Hill Steel Drum Band—
you can make it, all right!
—E.B.S.

ANTICIPATION...

It is said by those in the business,

"the only real musician is the amateur musician."

Dayshawn Mojica looked out the window as the bus crossed the Third Avenue Bridge in New York City. Minutes later the bus was traveling down the wide streets of Harlem. Even on this cold late-December day, people crowded the sidewalks. Shops selling everything from shoes and cell phones to T-shirts and vegetables lined the avenues.

How close are we? Dayshawn wondered. A street sign for Frederick Douglass Boulevard flashed by. Then suddenly, there it was, the world famous—*world famous*—Apollo Theater. This was the place where James Brown, Dionne Warwick, Bill Cosby, Stevie Wonder, D'Angelo, Dru Hill, and scores of other performers had gotten their starts.

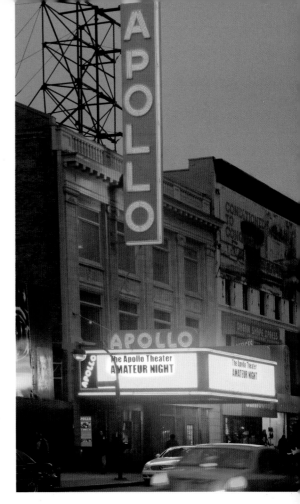

Dayshawn let out a whoop. The six other boys in the Hamilton Hill Steel Drum Band looked up from their naps or whispered conversations. They

had been traveling since dawn from Schenectady, in upstate New York. Now, with a busload of friends, teachers, relatives, and supporters, the boys were once again on their way to play in an Apollo competition. This would be their fourth time striding onto the stage, touching the good-luck Tree of Hope,

and playing their hearts out to the wild, enthusiastic audience. This would also be the final time, no matter if they won or lost. But they really wanted to win.

GETTING TOGETHER

The news spread fast. Talent scouts from the Apollo Theater were coming to town to hold an Apollo on Tour competition. These contests were being held around the country to let amateur artists compete for a chance to appear on the Apollo stage in the famous Amateur Night shows in New York City. The Schenectady Apollo on Tour show was going to be held at Proctors Theater, and the auditions would take place in just three weeks. One afternoon Miki Conn, director of the Hamilton Hill Arts Center, got a call. "Send those boys in the steel drum band on over," her friend said.

Miki called Ahmel and Aaron Williams and Spencer Anderson. Through the arts center the three boys had formed a steel drum band, and word had gotten around that they were good. "There's a problem though," Miki told them. "It's a big stage and the theater will be filled with people. You'll need a bigger band, a bigger sound."

The boys looked at the friends they hung out with at their high school, the John Sayles School of Fine Arts. They wanted really good musicians to join their band; but they also wanted friends who got their humor, their hassles, their serious sides, even their moods and anger.

They wanted guys they could grow with as musicians, musicians they could work with to write and play better songs. And they wanted to have fun.

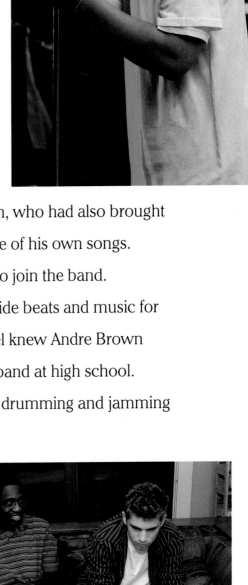

Dha'Sean Serrano was the best combination dancer-drummer in school. At a dance contest he had edged Ahmel out of first place by flipping and worming his way across the stage, but they became good friends anyway. Dha'Sean got a call to be in the band.

Dayshawn Mojica was a dancer also. One day Ahmel had seen a guy in the park doing the Harlem Shake like he had never seen it before. It was Dayshawn, who had also brought down the house at a talent show, wooing a girl with one of his own songs. Dayshawn was good on keyboards too. He was asked to join the band.

Steven Senisi had been working with Ahmel to provide beats and music for the raps Ahmel was writing. Aaron, Spencer, and Ahmel knew Andre Brown since middle school; and Steven met Andre in the jazz band at high school. Steven and Andre started an informal group and began drumming and jamming together. Both boys were naturals for the band.

The Hamilton Hill Steel Drum Band was in place. They were seven great musicians, and some were dynamite dancers too. The challenge would be to pull off a unified, unique, totally amazing sound in just a few weeks.

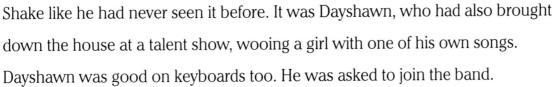

MEET THE BAND

"Young

AHMEL WILLIAMS

When Ahmel enters a room, he fills it with a vibe of *right here, right now, this is exactly where I want to be.* His grin is wide and friendly. He's about connections and positive energy, fun and competitiveness.

> **"**You got to have fun, aim high, don't ever settle. Just keep on going until you reach the most that you can ever get, and you just keep going after that.**"**

One day when Ahmel was nine he was in the basement computer lab of the Hamilton Hill Arts Center. A twangy sound wafted down the stairs. It was full, exotic, melodic—different from anything he had heard before.

Ahmel climbed the steps to the main floor to check out the sound. In the center of the room were two crazy-looking instruments. A man was leaning over one, hitting the concave sides with rubber-ended drumsticks. Each time he struck the instrument, a clear note traveled through the air. It was a beautiful sound, soft and full of vibrations twisting over and around each other. The man, musician John Joseph, invited Ahmel to play the other drum.

In school Ahmel also learned to play snare drums and saxophone. Piano and guitar he just picked up along the way. Today Ahmel is a rapper, singing about his life and experiences.

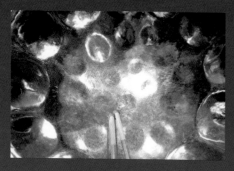

STEEL DRUMS (PANS)

Steel drums, also called pans, originated in Trinidad in the 1930s. They are made by repeatedly slamming a sledgehammer into the bottom of an empty, 55-gallon oil barrel, stretching the metal into the shape of a shallow soup bowl. This is called "sinking the pan."

In Trinidad, panmakers sometimes work on the beach. They build a fire and alternate scorching the pans and plunging them into the ocean to cool the red-hot metal. This tempers the steel for tuning. The notes are then gently pounded into the metal until they blend together. The finished instruments are either painted bright colors or coated with zinc or chromium to make them shiny.

Today steel drums are used all over the world——in rock groups, reggae bands, jazz combos, and more. Wherever they are played, steel drums give the music a rich, tropical Caribbean sound.

"Sometimes I get nervous. I won't know the right words to say to my friends or to people who don't know me, so I'll let them hear my music. I rap to inspire people to live better and for them to know there is nothing impossible to grab. All we have to do is reach. It's really easy for me to tell them through my music."

Ahmel also plays music by ear, listening to a recording and then heading to the arts center to pick out the tune on the piano. Once he has the melody, he figures out the beat, trying to unleash the power of the song, the catchy hook that will keep it in someone's head.

"dreamz"

AARON WILLIAMS

Growing up, every day was another adventure for Aaron as he tried to keep up with his older brothers, Ahmel and Spencer. The three boys were tight, and shared a passion for music, especially Aaron's favorites—rap duo Kris Kross, R&B group Soul 4 Real, and gospel singer Walt "Baby" Love.

The boys' grandfather was a pastor, and some of Aaron's strongest memories are of going to church. He loved watching his grandfather preach. After the services, Aaron was allowed to pound on the church's drums, picking out different rhythm patterns.

Along with Ahmel, Aaron was introduced to steel drums at the Hamilton Hill Arts Center. Then in elementary school he took a keyboard class.

> **❝My brother and I figured out how to play a song we heard on the radio. We matched the sound to the key and figured out what the note was. I was drawn to music. Music was what kept me going.❞**

To Aaron music is a language, a way of communicating his thoughts and feelings. He and his brothers have been speaking this language since they were young boys playing at being DJs with their father's old equipment.

JOHN SAYLES SCHOOL OF FINE ARTS

The John Sayles School of Fine Arts is a small learning community named for independent filmmaker John Sayles. The school, part of Schenectady High School, is dedicated to fostering academic exploration and immersing students in theater, dance, music, and visual and media arts. There is a nine-hundred seat auditorium, a smaller performance space known as a "black box theater," choir and band rooms, a dance studio, a computer graphics lab, a recording studio, and a section that houses a cable television program.

In addition to its strong academic curriculum, including the challenging International Baccalaureate Program, the school is designed to encourage students to take creative risks and test their talents in the arts. Some go on to performing arts schools, such as The Juilliard School in New York City and Berklee College of Music in Boston. The John Sayles school has a broader mission, however. It also aims to give students a lifelong appreciation of art, music, theater, dance, and creative expression of all kinds.

At school Aaron creates rhythms for the drumline, a marching group that plays percussion instruments, mostly drums. And recently he took the huge step of rapping his feelings for a girl at the school's talent show.

> **"**Last year I really liked this girl. I told her this by rapping the words at the talent show. Dayshawn was singing in the chorus, and I had my brother play the piano for me. I guess you could say music is a good way to explain things.**"**

When the steel drum band was just Aaron and his brothers, they knew only one song, *"Bailamos,"* which they were invited to play for a local television program. After that came a slew of invitations to play at functions around town. At each performance they played that song over and over, a little different every time, and the crowds loved it.

"E-Z

SPENCER ANDERSON

Spencer Anderson plays football and basketball, but he also has the sensibility of a writer. He has been writing poetry since he was a young boy. It helps him explain his world.

> **"**Poetry is overlooked. You're either a rapper or a singer in this community that I know of, so when people first hear me, they think, Oh, he's crazy. This is how a crazy man thinks.**"**

His father, Spencer Senior, left the Bronx to raise Spencer in upstate New York. There he met and married Wanda Byrd, who had Ahmel, Aaron, and daughters of her own. Spencer Senior worked as a DJ, and the boys loved to imitate him. He would put them on milk crates so they could reach the CD player. He gave them names: Ahmel was DJ-Crate, Aaron was DJ-Too Short, and Spencer was Spencer-D.

Spencer (left) with his father and Aaron

Music was everywhere in their home; but with a large family, private music lessons were not possible. One year Spencer Senior and Wanda gave each boy an instrument for Christmas. Spencer received an electric bass. Later he learned to play the steel drums at the arts center.

THE HAMILTON HILL ARTS CENTER

The Hamilton Hill Arts Center, located in the toughest neighborhood in Schenectady, is a popular gathering place for local kids. This is because of Miki Conn, the

center's director. Miki was active in the civil rights movement of the 1960s. During that time she learned that people could join together for positive change. This has inspired her work at the arts center, which she considers the biggest challenge of her life.

Miki relishes her role of mentoring children who walk through the center's doors. "I want them to be successful and happy and able to relate to all children," she says. She fills the center with painting and craft supplies, and covers the walls with the works of local artists. African dance is on the schedule; and classes in the *djembe*, a West African drum, are offered. Steel drums were added to bring in music from the Caribbean. And it was the steel drums that led to the most exciting thing that ever happened to kids from the arts center— the Apollo Theater competitions.

"I started playing because I always loved music. I loved it all the time. I could catch things by ear. Just show me the notes and let me hear the sounds. There were times I messed up, forgot what part was next. But after I knew the order of the song and where all the notes were, I pretty much had it."

Spencer is the quiet one in the family, a dreamer. He thinks carefully before he speaks. When he does speak, it is with a gravity and authority beyond his years. Although the band members can banter Spencer into a lighthearted mood, his real nature is to follow his own inner path, his own rhythms.

In their spare time, Spencer, Aaron, and Ahmel volunteer at the arts center, teaching young kids to play the steel drums.

"all
day

DAYSHAWN MOJICA

Singing and performing came naturally to Dayshawn. One Sunday when he was three years old, Dayshawn just belted out a song in church, which didn't seem at all odd to his family. His grandfather had a band in Georgia, and they traveled the world performing. Dayshawn also has a brother, uncles, and cousins who play drums, piano, electric bass, and sing solo or in groups.

Dayshawn (left) with his brother

> **"**It's like, all around you is music. All you hear all day long is music. That was the one real thing that my family was good at, so I would hear it every day. When you grow up around something so much, you can't let it go.**"**

In elementary school Dayshawn was often caught singing a song out loud and tapping his feet to a beat that just popped into his head. Church was different though. Church was where Dayshawn learned he could drum. He would watch the drummer, his uncle George, and clap his hands to the beat.

ROCKIN' AND ROLLIN' AT CHURCH

I went with Dayshawn to his church. There was a show in the basement. The first half was singing, and Dayshawn came on. At intermission they had a dance contest. The guys were wearing do-rags and baggy pants. It's a place where they could express themselves. A lot of kids from school were there. Families were there. Babies were there. It was Saturday night, and these kids weren't running around doing something crazy. Instead they were in church.

Pat Harmon, English teacher, John Sayles School of Fine Arts

"One day my uncle said to clap, clap, clap on a steady beat and, yeah, I could do that. Then he said to tap, tap, tap on a steady beat with my foot. I built up my strength, and that was when I really started drumming. Now I think about music all day long. I write a song two times a week."

When Dayshawn got the call to join Spencer, Ahmel, and Aaron in the Hamilton Hill Steel Drum Band, he felt good, even though at the time he didn't know what the Apollo Theater was. He started watching *Showtime at the Apollo* on television. He saw clips of Michael Jackson, Lauryn Hill, Alicia Keys, and others performing at the theater. He heard the legend about the famous black door that every performer has to pass before stepping onto the stage. All those people he had seen on television had walked by that door. Dayshawn was ready to join them.

"Asaph

ANDRE BROWN

Andre has a trapdoor song. It's "Summertime" by Will Smith. Whenever Andre hears this song, he goes through that door to the summer he was nine. He is at his grandmother's house, throwing water balloons at his cousins, playing cards with his aunts and uncles, helping his grandmother make fried chicken, catching fireflies with his sister.

When Andre was twelve, he and his mother moved to Birmingham, Alabama, while his father stayed in Schenectady. Missing the closeness of his extended family, Andre took up with the local kids, hanging out on the streets, smoking, and drinking. At age fifteen Andre moved back to Schenectady to live with his father. There Andre turned his back on the street life, and his immense energy went into music. One day he walked into music teacher Susan Cohen's beginning piano class. Even though he had never taken a lesson, he was soon accompanying students as they sang. Now Andre sings in three choirs and plays in five bands, but he is first of all a drummer.

"The only thing Andre likes more than playing drums is playing drums in front of a hundred people," said band leader Jason Hyatt. "He just shines as soon as he gets in front of people."

WHAT MAKES A GOOD DRUMMER?

You take the boys in the band—they are all extremely good drummers. They all have a very good sense of time. You have to have a good sense of time. You also have to have a good sense of rhythm, which is beyond a sense of time. Time is being able to stay on beat, and rhythm is understanding what is going on, what the piece is asking for rhythmically. And then it is whatever you can throw into it intuitively. That's the package of drumming. After that you have a thing called presence. Presence is that larger-than-life quality. You can't buy or teach it—you just have it.

Jason Hyatt, band leader and musician, John Sayles School of Fine Arts

Teachers talk about Andre's talent, and friends talk about his charisma. He slides into the leader position of any group he joins by saying at just the right moment, "Okay guys, we've got to get this thing together." Andre has learned from his friends too. He picked up electric bass from Steven and tapping from Dha'Sean.

In the end, Andre says it's music that saved him, and music is his future.

> **"**Music is what I want and what I need and what I am going to need to survive. If I don't make it big in the industry, I'll become a teacher, a mentor, for middle school or high school students. I want to share with them what I have been through.**"**

"Keyz

STEVEN SENISI

When Steven was three, he heard Beethoven's Ninth Symphony and fell in love with the catchy notes at the end. Some children drag around stuffed animals, blankets, or favorite toys. Steven walked around with earphones and his tape recorder, listening to Beethoven, over and over, for a year.

Steven grew up in a house with drums, keyboards, a piano, and many other instruments. He started playing the violin at age three, piano at five, and cello at eight. Then he went on to learn the electric bass.

Steven looked up to his older brother, Will, who was always jamming with friends, pounding out tunes, playing guitar and drums, and writing songs. Steven wanted to do all that. Then he got interested in rap and hip-hop, and wanted to learn to create beats for hip-hop songs using an electronic sequencer and a digital keyboard.

When Steven sits at a piano now, his hands fly over the keys, playing melodies he hears in his head. He is hoping to find a way to make the music work for him, to write and play songs because it is what he loves to do. Steven doesn't care about being famous. He wants to be free to create his own style, his own kind of music.

MAKING BEATS

Beats are the building blocks of hip-hop and rap music. Catchy melodies, sound effects, heavy basslines, and driving drum rhythms are elements of a beat that may be used in a hip-hop song. A performer raps or sings on top of and along with the beat.

Beats can be created using instruments, recording equipment, drum machine units, and computer software, or just with software, known as a computer-based sequencer. A composer uses this equipment and software to create sounds and rhythms that are layered on top of each other. The software also allows the composer to edit the layers separately and then mix them together in a variety of ways.

Making beats was once possible only in professional studios. Today newer, cheaper technology has made beat making a passion of amateurs and professionals alike.

"You can play something by accident and that's when you get songs. You just kind of slip up and, hey, that sounds good! Then you expand on that idea."

Musician Chick Corea is one of Steven's heroes. Chick played keyboards and wrote music for a group called Return to Forever. The jazz fusion they played, a mix of jazz and rock, often with some Spanish and a few other musical influences thrown in, has been a big inspiration to Steven. At age sixty Chick is still writing and playing with some of the best jazz musicians today.

"There are friendships in music. We don't have to say anything. We're just there in the music. No competition, no making fun—just expressing ourselves and connecting to each other through the music."

DHA'SEAN SERRANO

Born in New York City, Dha'Sean spent the first few years of his life surrounded by music and the musicians in his father's family. After Dha'Sean moved to Schenectady as a young boy, he started dancing and performing. He would race across the living room and shinny up the bookshelves. His father would run after him, arms outstretched, to catch his son; but Dha'Sean always landed on his feet. He had the balance, the moves. He had the gift.

Dha'Sean (left) with his brother

Dha'Sean took his first tap dance lessons when he was six years old. "It's drumming with your feet, just drumming and tapping," he'd tell his mother. He started playing real drums at age seven. The other instruments he plays, he just picked up on his own.

"I've been Mr. Teen America. I know kids look up to me. I'm cool with all kinds of kids. They look at me because of what I do, and I'm not afraid of doing it the way that I do."

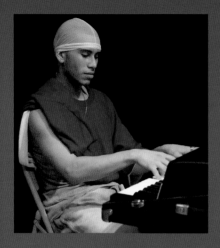

PLAYING BY EAR

"Playing by ear" refers to the ability to play a piece of music solely from hearing it, without looking at printed music or other notations. When a person plays by ear, the mind works to make sense of the tune he or she is hearing while the hands or lips work to put the tune on an instrument. Some musicians can play by ear, while others need the music in front of them.

The members of the Hamilton Hill Steel Drum Band can all play by ear. They listen to a song and then pick it out on their instruments. The boys also "play by ear" their own music—those original tunes, rhythms, and compositions they hear inside their heads.

Walking down the hallway in school between classes, Dha'Sean looks and talks like lots of other students, only maybe a little quieter, maybe even shy. But onstage, Dha'Sean is a different person. He can capture an audience. He feels the audience.

> **"**My parents and my teachers, they exposed me to everything. Each year we have competitions. You have to think that you are going to make it, that you are the best, because if you think down on yourself, you are going to be bad.**"**

In the band, Dha'Sean plays the *djembe*. But if the audience tells him to dance, if Dha'Sean can feel the connection, he slips away from the *djembe* and drums with his feet across the stage, to the beat of the steel drums and the rhythms he feels inside.

THE AUDITION
February 2005

When the band was just Ahmel, Aaron, and Spencer, they had learned to play the song *"Bailamos"* by ear. Now the seven boys did the same as a larger group. They listened to the song all the way through. Then they broke it down note by note and put it back together—their way.

"We knew we had to do something really big," said Andre. "We had to do flashy for the audition, with cuts and punches and breaks. We put our minds and hearts together and came up with a chorus and a verse. We put in breaks and solos to give everybody a chance to play. We ended with a drum solo that would really appeal to the audience."

The boys worked the song around Ahmel, Spencer, and Aaron on the steel drums, which carried the melody. Steven, on the electric bass, brought in the bassline, a low-pitched series of notes that kept the rhythm tight and solid. Dayshawn worked the keyboard, complementing the rhythm. Andre filled out the sound on the drum set, and Dha'Sean added the deep

throb of the *djembe*. The band was fluid, though, and the boys often switched instruments. But whenever they played *"Bailamos,"* they rocked the song hard.

The band had time for only one full rehearsal before the audition. They went off to the performance as if it were just a gig, never expecting the swarm of talent waiting backstage. Two hundred groups, most of them adult performers, were vying for twenty winning spots. It could have been a disaster, but the boys kept their cool. Having fun, more than winning, was on their minds.

From the start others knew that the band had something special. When the boys played, their sessions were electric. So when the band was selected as one of the twenty winners, no one was really surprised except the boys.

Next up—the Apollo on Tour show at Proctors Theater. The band had about a month to practice, but with their busy school and after-school job schedules, the boys were only able to squeeze in three rehearsals.

APOLLO ON TOUR AT PROCTORS

March 2005

The Apollo on Tour show at Proctors, unlike the audition, was open to the public. Audience participation was part of the show. The more clapping, cheering, shouting, and foot stomping performers got from the audience, the better their chances of winning. Only the winning act would go on to the Amateur Night competitions at the Apollo.

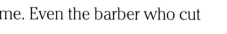

On the night of the performance, supporters came out in droves. Friends, family, and relatives came. The Hamilton Hill Arts Center crowd came. The high school crowd came. Other music-loving folks the band knew in the community came. Even the barber who cut some of the boys' hair came.

Under the beaming lights on Proctors' stage the band played *"Bailamos"* with the precision of seasoned performers. When they won, the crowd went wild. Everyone felt like a winner. People were hugging and screaming, "We won! We won!"

After the shock of winning washed over the boys, they stepped back and looked at one another. It was hard to describe the excitement that was surging through their bodies. The thrill was unbelievable.

The band members were now local celebrities. The newspaper wrote them up, and the television station had them on the news. The band was given an outstanding leadership award, a community pride award, and a letter of merit from the New York state legislature. And everyone wanted to follow the band to the Apollo Theater in New York City.

MEREDITH L. KAISER/GAZETTE PHOTOGRAPHER

Members of the Hamilton Hill Steel Drummers, Spencer Anderson, left, Ahmel Williams, Steve Sinisi, Dha'Sean Serrano and Aaron Williams, practice at the Hamilton Hill Arts Center in Schenectady. The group won the recent Apollo Theater talent contest at Proctor's.

Hamilton Hill Steel Drummers are heading to Harlem theater

BY PHILIP SCHWARTZ
Gazette Reporter

SCHENECTADY — The Hamilton Hill Steel Drummers, a group of seven teens from Schenectady, aren't exactly sure when they'll be performing at Harlem's venerable Apollo Theater.

And at this point, the *when* doesn't matter very much. The simple fact that it will be happening — that they'll take the same legendary stage that spawned the careers of greats like Billie Holiday, Ella Fitzgerald, James Brown and Lauryn Hill — is enough to sustain them.

The dream came true last Saturday when the touring version of Apollo's Amateur Night made its stop at Proctor's Theatre.

At that show, 20 acts competed before a crowd of 1,800-plus, who collectively acted as judge and picked the group as winners — the way all Apollo Amateur Night crowds do. Audience members cheer for who they think is the best act, and the Apollo's applause meter measures which one received the most cheers.

On Saturday, the winning act was the Hamilton Hill Steel Drummers — Spencer Anderson, 16, Ahmel Williams, 16, Aaron Williams, 14, Andre Brown, 17, Dha'Sean Serrano, 16, Steve Sinisi, 17, and the latest addition, Dayshawn Mojica.

LARGEST AUDIENCE

Before Saturday, the band had never played in front of an audience 1,800 strong. And now, after hearing it, they speak of the roar of the crowd as an elixir.

"I've never heard a crowd so loud, unless it was for a celebrity," Ahmel Williams said Monday after the Steel Drummers rehearsed at the Hamilton Hill Arts Center.

But the opportunity to perform at the Apollo may come with some mild trepidation — though band members joked about it at their rehearsal.

A CRAZED CLOWN

Like at the Proctor's show, the Apollo audience is encouraged to boo off any acts they don't like. And their heckling brings out the "Executioner," a crazed clown carrying om, who sweeps the

heckled off stage. At Proctor's, the crowd brought out the Executioner seven times. Knowing this, the Hamilton Hill Steel Drummers also understand that a Harlem audience is more discriminating. Hence, the trepidation.

"If they didn't hold back in Schenectady, they sure ain't going to hold back in Harlem," Serrano joked.

Yet, band members agree that their chances of getting booed off in Harlem are slim.

This road to the Apollo started last month when approximately 200 performers showed up at Proctor's for an initial tryout. Twenty made the first cut and performed on Saturday, leaving the Steel Drummers as the last act standing — the act that makes the trip to Harlem to a theater none of the seven has even stepped foot in.

"We've passed [the Apollo] before on trips to New York," Ahmel Williams said. "But we've never been there. The fact that we have the opportunity to go is amazing."

APOLLO

The Apollo Theater
AMATEUR NIGHT

April & September 2005

The first of the three Amateur Night competitions at the Apollo Theater was scheduled for early April. The band had to compete with contest winners from across the nation and be voted one of the top acts in all three competitions—Apollo on Tour, Show-Off, and Top Dog—to qualify for the Super Top Dog competition in late December. The performances would be in front of the Amateur Night crowd, on the Apollo stage, "where stars are born and legends are made." These would be much tougher audiences than the one at Proctors.

Miki Conn sent out fliers and made calls to gather support for the band. With Wanda Byrd's help, Miki hired buses and sold tickets for the ride to New York City. The audience chooses the winners and losers, so the band wanted to pack a section of the theater with friends and family who would raise the roof for them. They needed their fans to stomp, clap, and shout their approval—and send the needle of the "clap-o-meter," a device that measures audience participation, off the charts. They especially didn't want to get booed off the stage, which the Apollo allows and even encourages if the audience doesn't like an act.

Early on a damp, chilly morning in April, three buses barreled down Highway 87, headed for the Apollo on Tour competition. Four hours later, when the buses turned on

THE APOLLO THEATER

The Apollo Theater opened in 1913 in Harlem as an all-white music hall. In the 1920s Harlem transformed into a black neighborhood. Then in 1934, under new management, the Apollo became a theater for black performers and audiences. Every major black star since that time has appeared on the Apollo stage.

The Apollo has an aura and a mystique that goes far beyond its elegant old building. In 1983 the theater was designated as a New York City landmark, and today it is a top tourist attraction. Part of the theater's popularity comes from the Amateur Night shows, started more than seventy years ago; the Top Dog competitions; and the television show *Showtime at the Apollo*.

The Apollo helped launch the careers of Ella Fitzgerald, Billie Holiday, Pearl Bailey, Stevie Wonder, and countless others. For both emerging and established performers, it doesn't get any better than playing the Apollo and winning the Apollo crowd.

THE GREEN ROOM

The green room is the space where performers wait before taking the stage in theaters, television studios, and many other performance venues.

For hundreds of years actors and other performers have waited to go onstage in a green room. The term first appeared in written English in 1701, but its origin is unknown. Some say it comes from medieval times, when plays were often staged on "the green," a grassy meadow, surrounded by spectators. Others say the term originated in Shakespeare's day, when actors changed costumes and waited in a room filled with green plants, which were thought to keep the air moist and actors' voices full. Still others say early waiting rooms for actors were in fact painted green, although no one is sure why this color was chosen.

to West 125 Street in Manhattan, the boys looked up in awe at the theater marquee. The huge neon-bright letters forming the word APOLLO were a shiny symbol of opportunity to the band members. Maybe they too would make history on the Apollo stage.

Once inside, the boys walked silently through the long red lobby. They stopped at a wall plastered with a photographic mural of entertainers who had played the Apollo. Then, pushing through the doors at the end of the lobby, the boys found themselves staring at the stage at the front of the theater. With the houselights on, the stage could have looked ordinary, even a bit scruffy. But the band members knew the rich history that elevated the worn floor and heavy curtains to legendary status. This was a stage of possibilities and dreams.

The band was ushered down narrow concrete steps to the green room. The boys settled in a corner near a door, waiting until they were called onstage for a sound check. They were aching to get their hands on the house band's equipment.

When their turn came to adjust the sound for their performance, the boys were amazed at how the professional instruments played, how their music filled the huge theater with its two balconies and rows and rows of red seats.

"It's a whole different thing on the Apollo stage," said Steven. "I'm using a bass player's bass and amp, the whole stack. And we are being blasted through the PA system. It's like, hard-core."

"I'm really holding this guy's drumsticks," said Andre, "this guy I've been watching on TV holding these same drumsticks. It's incredible. There's no other feeling like it. Your heart's racing. Your adrenalin's pumping."

After the sound check, the band settled in the front row of the theater, watching the other acts test the instruments. There were also dancers and singers and rappers. There weren't a lot of bands. Maybe steel drums were something different, the band hoped, something the Apollo crowd hadn't seen before.

Back in the green room, the boys were wired tight as they waited for their performance of *"Bailamos."* When the show's producer, Vanessa Brown,

entered the room, all eyes focused on her. "Next up, the Hamilton Hill Steel Drum Band," she announced. "Line up outside at the top of the steps."

At the top of the stairway, just offstage, was a black door leading to a small office.

Over the years, as performers stood there, several had written their names on the door. The boys traced some of the famous names with their fingers, wondering if those performers had felt as excited and nervous as they did now.

Just then Capone, the host for Amateur Night, called the band onstage. Each band member touched the Tree of Hope and strode across the stage to his place. Giving one another nods, as easy as that, the boys started playing. "When it was our turn, we just went up there and did what we do best," said Ahmel.

Even before the song was over, an electrifying charge surged through the audience as the band's families, friends, and fans roared their approval. The clap-o-meter went wild. Then, after all the performers were finished, everyone was called back onstage. As each act stepped forward, the clap-o-meter measured the audience's response. The Apollo crowd clapped and stomped the Hamilton Hill Steel Drum Band to second place! The band would be back later in April for the Amateur Night Show-Off competition.

THE TREE OF HOPE

Touching the Tree of Hope on the Apollo stage is an Amateur Night tradition. The Tree of Hope is actually a log. It was cut from a tree that originally stood near the old Lafayette Theater on Seventh Avenue in Harlem. The tree was a gathering place for show business people and eventually became a symbol of good luck for all who stood under its branches. In 1934 New York City widened Seventh Avenue, and the tree was one of many that were cut down. It was cut into logs and sold as souvenirs, one of which was bought by Ralph Cooper Sr., founder of the Apollo Amateur Night competitions. He had the log placed onstage to bring good luck to all who performed there. The Tree of Hope now links performers past and present in their quest for success.

For the next trip to the Apollo, the boys knew the routine. They ran onstage, touched the Tree of Hope, and played with total confidence, breaking open *"Bailamos"* so that it sounded new and fresh and wild. Dha'Sean, feeling especially connected to the audience, left the *djembe* to tap and flip across the stage. Once again the audience screamed and applauded loudly for the band.

Back in the green room, waiting for the other acts to finish, the boys felt good about their performance. Still, their faces were tense as they walked up the stairs and onto the stage for judging. Either the excited frenzy of the audience would catapult them to the next round or the booing would send them offstage, helped along by CP Lacey, the "executioner," who would race onto the stage in one of his colorful costumes and chase them off.

The boys stepped forward when the band's name was called, and the clap-o-meter went crazy. The band came in second, which qualified them to return to the Apollo Theater in September for Top Dog, the competition where two-time winners compete against other two-time winners.

In September the Apollo crowd cheered and stomped and clapped the band to one of the winning spots in the Top Dog contest. The boys knew they had made it almost to the top. The Hamilton Hill Steel Drum Band was on its way to the final round—the Super Top Dog competition.

SUPER TOP DOG

December 28, 2005

As the bus pulled up to the Apollo Theater on that cold December day, the thrill of the upcoming performance took hold of the boys. It was in their eyes and in the way they continually tapped rhythms with their fingers. They were going for Super Top Dog.

"Word was we had to wait on the bus for a while. But we grabbed our gear and our outfits, and we were like— let's go do this!" said Andre. "We got off the bus. The Apollo people treated us like royalty. We felt like stars. It was just so incredible. We were triggered. It was crazy."

The Apollo Theater
AMATEUR NIGHT

NO STANDING
ANYTIME
EXCEPT VEHICLES WITH
LICENSE
NYP PLATES
→

NO PARKING

In the green room the boys claimed their corner for the long night ahead. They stuffed duffel bags under the seats and hung ironed shirts from the backs of chairs. When it was time for the sound check of the equipment, they waited upstairs in the theater, where spotlights passing over the stage flashed rose and lime green and psychedelic blue. The band members quietly watched the competing acts. These performers were good, and for the first time a wave of doubt swept over the boys. What made them think they could do this, compete with some of the best amateurs in the country? But just then the band was called onstage. There wasn't time to panic.

After the sound check, back in the green room, conversations were whispered. Everyone was trying to stay cool and focused. At one point an assistant to the show's producer clip-clopped into the room in high-heeled boots. "By seven fifteen we need you dressed, sharp, and ready to go," she announced, handing out numbered cards showing the order of the lineup. "But first we pray together. Who would like to lead?"

Ahmel bowed his head and started a prayer familiar to the band. "Guide our hands and our hearts," he began. "Make us better than we are. Keep us humble and help us grow at the same time." By the time they were done, all the performers in the room had bowed their heads and clasped hands. Thoughts were focused on Ahmel's quiet meditation.

Then Ahmel broke the spell. "Hey, how many winners are there?" he called out.

"For Super Top Dog there is only one winner," the assistant said. "That act goes on to the television show *Showtime at the Apollo* and wins some money. But remember, just being here makes you a winner."

Then the assistant was gone, only to return a short while later with rules. "When we call your number, line up on the steps by the black door. Touch the Tree of Hope when you get onstage. When you leave, even if CP Lacey is chasing you off with a popgun, turn to the audience and say, 'Thank you, Apollo.'" She paused, then added, "Don't believe in your dreams. Make your dreams believe in you."

A murmur went through the green room as everyone settled back into his or her private thoughts. Tension mounted, and performers eyed the other acts, trying to judge how good they were.

Dayshawn looked around the room. "Hey, everyone is too serious here," he shouted. "Now I'm feelin' a show. Let's just relax and let it go."

In the theater the house band struck a loud chord. Capone strode onstage to screams and cheers as the lights swung colorful arcs into the

PLAYING THE APOLLO

All these performers, and numerous others, appeared in Amateur Night competitions. Many won. Some did not. Many became famous national or international stars. Some did not. But when they first performed on the Apollo stage, they all experienced the thrill of "playing the Apollo," the nation's most popular venue for emerging entertainers.

1934 Ella Fitzgerald *vocalist*

1935 Billie Holiday *vocalist*

1942 Sarah Vaughan *vocalist*

1955 Joe Tex *vocalist*

1956 James Brown *vocalist*

1965 Gladys Knight & the Pips *vocal group*

1969 Michael Jackson / The Jackson 5 *vocal group*

1986 David Peaston *gospel singer*

1988 Lauryn Hill *vocalist*

1989 Dave Chappelle *comedian*

1990 Watson Sisters *vocalists*

1992 D'Angelo *vocalist*

1992 Dru Hill *vocal group*

audience. "These are the stars of tomorrow," he announced. His voice rang through the theater. "If you like what you hear, what should you do?"

The deafening applause and foot stomping from the audience were the answer. Then Capone asked the crowd to wait with any booing until the act had a fair chance. "We judge by talent, not race, not color, not clothing." Shouts and screams filled the theater. The audience was ready.

When the band's number was finally called, the boys moved up the steps and past the black door. Standing just offstage they held hands and bowed their

heads. All they could do was try to reach inside themselves for a calm, sure place. Quietly each boy made the mental switch from high school band to one of the top Apollo amateur acts.

"And now the Hamilton Hill Steel Drum Band from Schenectady, New York!" boomed Capone. As Capone's voice trailed off and the applause started, the boys ran onstage. After touching the Tree of Hope, they fanned out to their places under the hot stage lights. So many months of planning and practicing and dreaming walked onto that stage too.

Spencer and Aaron were on the steel drums. Steven played the electric bass. Dayshawn held down the keyboard. Andre covered the drum set and Dha'Sean the snare drums. Ahmel kept the beat on the *djembe*. The music was magical, washing over the audience in the rows of red seats. The band's rendition of *"Bailamos"* was layered and deep. It pulsed with the best the boys could give. Ahmel left the *djembe* and tapped until Dha'Sean came forward, flipping across the stage. The dancing and flipping were unrehearsed; but the boys kept playing, kept the sound going. They were thinking and moving in unison.

In less than five minutes the band's performance was over. The boys ran offstage to the sweet sounds of shouting and clapping. "Performing in front of the Apollo crowd was just wow!" said Aaron. "All you see is the front row of people, because there is this big glint of light shining on you. But you can hear the crowd, hear people cheering for you, feel people liking your music."

Reaching the green room, the boys breathed big sighs of relief. They had played well, kept up the beat, kept the music fresh. No one had booed. CP Lacey had stayed in the wings.

After the last performance all the acts crowded onstage. As Capone called them forward one by one, the audience erupted into clapping and cheering, and the clap-o-meter needle soared. "We were hoping. We were praying. We were scared," said Andre. When the Hamilton Hill Steel Drum band came forward, the boys heard applause, lots of applause, and cheering and stomping.

Even before Capone thanked all the performers and formally announced the winner, it was pretty clear who had sent the needle the highest. A fifteen-year-old singer was Super Top Dog for 2005. Onstage, the boys clapped for the winner. Offstage they felt pretty beat-up.

"After we lost I cried," said Ahmel.

"It was hard to believe," said Spencer. "We put in all that work, since February. And Ahmel and Aaron and I had been doing this for six years."

"It hurt. It really hurt," said Andre. "We didn't know what to do when

they didn't say our name. But we did our best. Just to be able to go through all that and go that far, it was incredible."

"The loss was hard," said Aaron. "But performing on the Apollo stage was a real great feeling. I couldn't get enough of that feeling, being on that stage."

Family, friends, and supporters crowded into the green room. "Hey, guys, you did well," Spencer Senior called, a big smile on his face. "What a show! What an experience you gave us. What an experience this has been for you."

Late that night, as the bus rumbled over the Willis Avenue Bridge and sped toward home, the boys were deep in their own thoughts. They absorbed the loss and disappointment, and reflected on all that had happened in the past year. Perhaps some were dreaming of returning to the Apollo years down the line, when they had made it as a drummer, a dancer, a rapper—or as a dad, cheering on his own son or daughter in an Amateur Night competition.

For the members of the Hamilton Hill Steel Drum Band, their time at the Apollo Theater will always be a part of their lives. Their dream of winning Super Top Dog did not come true, but a different dream was realized that night—a dream filled with the irrepressible joy of good friends making music together on the worn and wonderful, world famous Apollo stage.

"The Apollo experience was really all we needed," said Dha'Sean. "As far as everything else, we're all going to make it, every one of us."

STEEL DRUMMING AT THE APOLLO

SELECTIONS AVAILABLE

Total running time: 22:54

For free download please visit:

leeandlow.com/books/2453

1. **Bailamos** / *Paul Barry and Mark Taylor • 4:35*
   Performed by Hamilton Hill Steel Drum Band
   Spencer Anderson: *Double steel drums*
   Andre Brown: *Keyboards*
   Dayshawn Mojica: *Drum set*
   Steven Senisi: *Electric bass*
   Dha'Sean Serrano: *Djembe*
   Aaron Williams: *Single steel drum*
   Ahmel Williams: *Single steel drum, djembe*

2. **You Can Make It** / *Andre Brown • 3:44*
   Andre Brown: *Lyrics, music composition, keyboards*
   Dayshawn Mojica: *Drum set*
   Dayvon Mojica: *Vocals*
   Steven Senisi: *Electric bass*
   Will Senisi: *Electric guitar*

3. **Flow** / *Ahmel Williams • 3:10*
   Ahmel Williams: *Lyrics, vocals*
   Andre Brown: *Drum set*
   Steven Senisi: *Music composition, electric piano,
        electric bass, acoustic guitar*
   Dha'Sean Serrano: *Music composition*

4. **Breakdown 3:24 AM (Dedicated to Oshe)** /
    Steven Senisi • 3:03
   Steven Senisi: *Music composition, acoustic piano,
        electric piano, electric bass, drum set,
        analog synthesizer*
   Will Senisi: *Electric guitar*

5. **The Beauty of Words** / *Spencer Anderson • 1:31*
   Spencer Anderson: *Spoken word (poetry)*
   Steven Senisi: *Music composition, acoustic piano,
        electric piano, drum set, analog
        synthesizer, sequenced violin
        and drums*
   Will Senisi: *Electric guitar*

6. **A True Story** / *Dha'Sean Serrano • 1:33*
   Dha'Sean Serrano: *Music composition,
        sequenced beat*
   Steven Senisi: *Acoustic piano*

7. **The Love of Music** / *Dayshawn Mojica • 2:13*
   Dayshawn Mojica: *Lyrics, music composition,
        vocals, keyboards, electric bass,
        drum set*
   Will Senisi: *Electric guitar*

8. **Just Push** / *Aaron Williams • 3:05*
   Aaron Williams: *Lyrics, vocals*
   Steven Senisi: *Music composition, electric piano,
        sequenced beat*

Bailamos published by Crosstown Songs UK Ltd. (PRS);
  Sub-published by Fintage Publishing and Collection B.V.

Music recorded at DreamSpun Recording Group, Schenectady,
  New York

Mixed by Danny Lee and Steven Senisi at DreamSpun
  Recording Group

Mastered by Art Snay at Arabellum Studios, Albany, New York